Why
Are People
Prejudiced?

Cath Senker

**RAINTREE
STECK-VAUGHN
PUBLISHERS**

A Harcourt Company

Austin   New York
www.raintreesteckvaughn.com

Published by Raintree Steck-Vaughn Publishers, an imprint of Steck-Vaughn Company

Library of Congress Cataloging-in-Publication Data is available upon request.

ISBN 0-7398-4959-X

Printed in Italy. Bound in the United States.
1 2 3 4 5 6 7 8 9 0 06 05 04 03 02

Picture Acknowledgments
AKG London 16; Associated Press 22 (Charles Dharapak), 25 (Eddie Adams), 39; The Bridgeman Art Library 13; Camera Press 8, 24, 34, 42; Corbis 36 (Sandy Felsenthal); Howard J. Davies 27; Paul Doyle 4, 45; Robert Harding Picture Library 12; Hodder Wayland Picture Library 19 (J. Wright), 37 (top) (David Cumming); Panos Pictures *(imprint page)* (David Reed), 6 (Betty Press), 28 (Betty Press), 33 (David Reed), 35 (Penny Tweedie); Popperfoto *(contents)* (bottom), 9 (Adrees Latif, Reuters), 18 (Rula Halawani, Reuters), 21 (Petr Josek, Reuters), 23 (Mike Theiler, Reuters), 29 (Mike Theiler, Reuters), 30 (Jerry Lampen, Reuters), 38 (Achim Bieniek, Reuters), 40, 41 (Juda Ngwenya, Reuters), 43, 44 (Bob Thomas); Still Pictures 17 (Hartmut Schwarzbach); Topham Picturepoint *(cover)* (Nancy Richmond/The Image Works, *(contents)* (top), 5 (Jacksonville Journal Courier/The Image Works), 7 (Adrian Murrell), 10, 11, 14, 15, 20, 26, 31 (Jeff Greenberg/The Image Works), 32.

Contents

1. What Is Prejudice?

What Is Race?

Some people say that human beings can be divided into separate races. They believe that the various races look different and have different characteristics: for instance, some are smart, while others are good at sports.

These ideas about race became popular in Europe in the 18th and 19th centuries. For example, in the 19th century, a man named Count Arthur Gobineau wrote that history was a struggle between three races, the yellow, the black, and the white. He thought that the white race was superior and would win this struggle. Other writers believed that there were five races, not three. But even in those days, there were still people who believed there was only one race: the human race.

> **FACT:**
> The differences in skin color are controlled by just six genes out of a total of 100,000 in the human body. A person's height, on the other hand, is controlled by dozens of genes.

◀ *Schoolchildren at a girls' school in London, England. Unfortunately, most people are exposed to ideas about race at an early age.*

The science of genetics has proven that the idea of separate races is false. Skin color has always been seen as an indicator of a person's race. However, differences in skin color evolved many thousands of years ago when humans adapted to various climates and environments. People of different colors do not differ in significant ways genetically.

Yet the belief in separate races remains powerful. Some people are proud of their skin color; some people suffer as a result of their skin color. Mistaken ideas about race—including the belief that there is such a thing as race—help lead to prejudice.

"A white child of my acquaintance said to his black schoolmate, 'I wish I was black so I could play basketball as well as you.' The black child was offended and told his parents about the remark…. We often hear this kind of reasoning: 'Everyone I see playing basketball is black. Everyone playing basketball must be black. If I am not black, I can't play basketball; if you are black, you must be a basketball player.'"

Patricia Williams, Race and Race Relations Lecture, BBC

▲ *Some people believe that African Americans are "naturally" good at sports. This fails to recognize the hard work and effort necessary to develop the technique and specific skills to become a top athlete. The color of someone's skin can never ensure a person's success in sports—or anything else, for that matter.*

5

What Is Prejudice?

When people think badly of or say things about a particular group of people for no just reason, this is called prejudice. To have a prejudice means to pre-judge someone—to make up your mind about a person before you know anything about him or her. People can be prejudiced against others for various reasons. For example, some people hate beggars on the street because they think they are too lazy to work. Some are prejudiced against people from a different ethnic group, a set of people who share a different common culture, traditions, and sometimes language.

▼ A family at a shelter for homeless people in Florida. "Mixed" families are often victims of racism from many different groups. This can make it difficult for them to get a job or rent or buy a home.

Prejudice against a particular group can be directed toward various characteristics, including skin color, ethnicity, religion, or culture, this is called racism. People can be racist toward others because of what they think they are like, even if it is not true. For example, some people say that all Polish people are stupid and make jokes about them. This is just one example of prejudice.

◀ *Aborigine children outside a ruined house. Many Aborigines are so poor that they have to live in tin huts or shacks.*

When racism in society is directed toward a group of people, it can take opportunities away from them. Aborigines lived in Australia long before Europeans arrived there. Like Native Americans in the Americas, Aborigines were badly mistreated by Europeans because of the color of their skin and "primitive" ways. Today, they are still treated worse than other people in Australia. For example, it is difficult for them to get into a good school or to find a decent job. They are also more likely to be sent to prison for committing a crime, and for a longer period of time. These are examples of what is called "discrimination."

Although racism is no longer considered socially acceptable in most places, it continues to be a major problem in many societies throughout the world.

> Article 2: Everyone should have the rights outlined in the Universal Declaration whatever their ethnic group, sex, nationality, religion, political opinion, social group, ability, or wealth.
> *The Universal Declaration of Human Rights in simple language, Refugee Council, UK, 1998*

Forms of Prejudice

There are different forms of prejudice and it shows itself in various ways. People may experience:

- Others who express prejudiced views
- Name-calling and jokes
- Harassment
- Violence
- Organized discrimination by political parties
- Institutional racism

Some people with prejudiced views may keep them to themselves. They may never share them with other people. Others might laugh at racist jokes and pass them on, but they do not believe they are doing any real harm.

In the classroom, you might hear racist nicknames being used. Some of the people using them might think it's funny and that they are not really hurting anyone. But prejudice is harmful and frightening for those who suffer the insults.

▲ *In the 1970s the racist National Front in Great Britain organized marches through black areas. Here they have destroyed Asian people's shops in East London.*

In July 2001, in Brooklyn, New York, a few young people drew racist slogans and symbols on and around homes owned by Jews. Although none of the victims were physically attacked, they were very frightened and found it difficult afterward to feel safe in their own homes.

Sometimes violence is used. Racists may take out their hatred on one person they find on the street or attack a hostel where refugees live. For example, in June 2000, three racist "skinheads" in Dessau, Germany, murdered Alberto Adriano, an immigrant from Mozambique, Africa, because he was a "foreigner."

In many countries there are racist political organizations that try to gain support for their ideas. The Ku Klux Klan, a racist group formed by white Americans in the 19th century, still campaigns today against African Americans, Koreans, Jews, and other groups. In the worst cases, racist organizations may get into power and try to kill all the people in the group they hate. This is what happened under Hitler's Nazi regime during World War II.

> "On the night of June 11, three young skinheads drank vast quantities of alcohol, and roamed rowdily through the town's park. They beat the black African, Alberto Adriano, for such a long time and so mercilessly that he died of severe injuries in the hospital three days later."
>
> Bremer Nachrichten, *German newspaper, (translated), August 23, 2000*

▼ *Ku Klux Klan members demonstrate for the execution of Gary Graham, an African American who many people believe was wrongly convicted of murder.*

2. Historical Reasons for Prejudice

Where Does Prejudice Come From?

Throughout the history of the ancient and medieval worlds, various kinds of prejudice were common. They were not always based on skin color; for example, some Roman emperors were black. But people were often prejudiced against foreigners and minority groups who led a different way of life.

People often did not trust visitors from other places, because their customs were different. Since few people traveled from place to place in the same country, even people from another part of the same country were considered "foreigners." There was a marked dislike or even hatred of people from another land. This prejudice against outsiders is called xenophobia (from the Ancient Greek word meaning "fear of strangers").

The Roma, or Gypsies, are travelers. They left India in about the 10th century and have moved around the world ever since. Settled people have often distrusted them and blamed them for crime. This has been their excuse to hate and attack the Roma as "outsiders."

▼ *Roma, or Gypsies, leaving Hurtwood Hill in Surrey, England, in 1934. They had been living in the settlement for 100 years.*

A racist spraying a Nazi swastika on a wall in Belgrade, Serbia, in 1997. There is still a lot of anti-Semitism in eastern Europe today.

Throughout history, the Jews have suffered terrible prejudice. When prejudice is directed against Jews it is called anti-Semitism. In medieval times they were abused and often forced out of their countries. In Europe, Christians saw them as the killers of Christ. At times, such as in 15th-century Spain, Christian governments tried to force the Jews to become Christians. They would accept them only if they gave up their religion and culture. The most horrible example of Anti-Semitism was during World War II, when Adolf Hitler sought what he called "The Final Solution"— murdering all of the Jews who lived in Germany and Europe.

In colonial times, during the 18th and 19th centuries, these early forms of prejudice turned into a new kind of hatred based on ideas about "race."

FACT:
In the Middle Ages, many western European countries passed laws to throw out all Jewish people. Jews were forced out of England in 1290, France in 1394, and Spain in 1492.
A Historical Atlas of the Jewish People, 1992

Colonialism and Slavery

Over 400 years ago, powerful European nations sent ships and soldiers to other parts of the world and began to rule over the countries they discovered. This was the beginning of colonialism, and it led to new ideas about "race."

The colonists who took over the Caribbean, and North, Central, and South America from the 17th century onward needed workers for their farms. They brought millions of Africans as slaves; racist ideas made this trade seem acceptable to them. Africans were seen as no better than animals, or children who needed supervision.

FACT:
About 12 million Africans were torn from their homes and taken across the Atlantic Ocean as slaves. More than one in ten died on the way. Those who survived were sold and then forced to work up to eighteen hours a day.
Robin Blackburn, The Making of New World Slavery, 1997

◀ *A late 18th-century painting of slaves in North America. Here they may look relaxed, but in fact their lives were extremely hard and they had almost no free time.*

In some countries, such as South Africa, Europeans took control of the land and made local Africans work for them. Colonists also took over parts of Asia, Africa, and South America. Few of them settled there permanently, but their governments ruled the countries as colonies. The Europeans claimed that the native peoples were not able to govern themselves.

Europeans also settled in places such as Australia, New Zealand, and North America. They thought they were better than the native peoples. For example, Native Americans were seen as "primitive" because they wore animal skins and roamed the land. Some people today still believe that white European people are superior to everyone else.

A portrait of Olaudah Equiano. In England he joined the campaign against the slave trade.

case study · case study · case study · cas

In 1756, Olaudah Equiano was kidnapped from his village in Nigeria. He was 11 years old. An African blacksmith took him as a slave. Olaudah had several other African owners before being sent on a slave ship to Barbados in the Caribbean. He was then taken to Virginia, in North America, and forced to work on a tobacco plantation. A naval captain bought him next, and he spent several years at sea. In 1766, Equiano bought his freedom. Working as a sailor, he had many adventures. In Italy he saw the volcano Vesuvius erupt, he narrowly escaped being made a slave again in the United States, and he was shipwrecked in the Bahamas. Equiano moved to England and in 1789 published his autobiography entitled *The Interesting Narrative of the Life of Olaudah Equiano*. The book became a bestseller in England and an important voice for the abolishment of slavery.

Fascism

In the 1920s and 1930s some countries, such as Italy, Spain, and Germany, came under fascist rule. Fascists believed their nation was superior to others. Ruled by a powerful leader or dictator, they discriminated against people from other countries, cultures, or religions, and used force to conquer other countries. Fascist governments had the support of the mass of the population who were neither rich nor poor. These were people who felt powerless between the influence of big business on the one hand, and the workers in their trade unions on the other hand.

The Nazi government in Germany was the most racist of the fascist powers. Its leader, Adolf Hitler, believed that "Aryans"—blue-eyed Germans and Scandi-navians—were a superior race. Other races, such as the Slavs and Africans, were fit only to be slaves. Worst of all were the Jews; all Germany's problems were blamed on them.

▼ *An elderly Jewish man being stopped by Nazis in Berlin, Germany, in 1933.*

```
                FACT:
    The Jewish population before
World War II and the approximate
    numbers killed in eastern
       European countries:
                    Before      Killed
Poland          3,250,000   3,000,000
USSR            2,800,000   1,200,000
Romania           800,000     350,000
Hungary           400,000     300,000
Czechoslovakia    315,000     270,000
    A Historical Atlas of the Jewish
            People, 1992
```

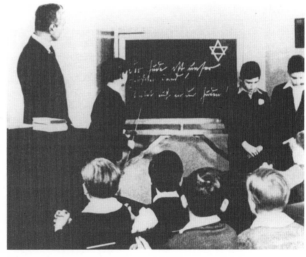

▼ *Two Jewish boys being ridiculed in their classroom in Nazi Germany in the early 1930s. Underneath the Star of David on the board it says, "The Jew is our greatest enemy. Beware of the Jew."*

During World War II, the Nazis wanted to kill all the Jews in Europe. In 1941 they built death camps in Poland, where they used poison gas to murder thousands of Jews every day. Millions of other people hated by the Nazis, such as Roma, Poles, Russians, homosexuals, and disabled people, were also killed.

There was racism in the countries that fought against Hitler, too. A fascist party tried to gain influence in Great Britain before World War II. Racism in the United States meant that black and white people lived separate lives as a result of segregation. After the war, many people felt that racism was bad. But the ideas did not die away altogether.

3. The Fear of the Unknown

How Can Ignorance Spread Prejudice?

When people don't know anything about another country or culture, they may believe false ideas that they have heard about it. They build up a picture in their heads about that culture —usually a negative one—and think bad things about all the people who belong to it.

When you think that something is true of a whole group of people, this is a stereotype. People can be stereotyped because of their sex—for example, "All men are strong"—or their age,—"All children are noisy." Stereotypes are not based on fact and they are usually insulting. They mean you are not looking at a person as an individual.

Sometimes people are stereotyped because they have a different skin color, culture, or religion. Things may be said about a group of people that are true of only some of them, for instance, "All Jews are rich." Most Jews are not rich, so this is an example of a stereotype that continues the cycle of prejudice.

▼ A poster for an anti-Semitic exhibition in Munich, Germany, in 1937. It shows a stereotype of a Jewish person, who was believed to be interested only in money.

Things may be said that are not true at all. Some people believe that people who wear turbans are dirty. They have the mistaken belief that people wear turbans to cover their dirty hair. However, none of this is true. People who wear turbans do so for religious reasons. There are many religions in the world that require people to cover their head or cut or wear their hair in a specific way. To make a value judgment about a person's or group's cultural practices, especially without understanding the reason for these practices, is one of the most common forms of prejudice.

But those people do not know about Asian culture because they are ignorant. They believe their own ways are better. Often they try to pass on their closed, stereotyped view of "dirty Asians" to other people. This is how racist ideas can spread.

"During a lesson on Kenya a class was shown a set of slides of Nairobi city center, with its skyscrapers and modern office blocks. Yet when asked what they noticed, the first thing they mentioned was a beggar, hardly visible, in the corner of one of the slides."

Angela Grunsell and Ros Wade, "Multicultural Teaching to Combat Racism in School and Community," 1995

▲ *A photo of Nairobi, Kenya, showing the city's modern office buildings and a wealthy Kenyan. It is not true that everyone in African countries is poor and lives in a village.*

Cultural Differences

Sometimes people are prejudiced toward another ethnic group. An ethnic group is a community of people who share the same culture, and often the same language. For example, immigrants in the United States may speak their own language at home, follow their own customs, and eat different types of food from most people around them. Some Americans may say that this group does not fit into their society because it has a "foreign" way of life.

Prejudice can often be linked to religion, too. For example, it has been said that Muslim Asians in Western countries suffer from "double prejudice." They are discriminated against because of the color of their skin, and also because they practice Islam.

▼ *Muslims praying in front of the Dome of the Rock in Jerusalem. The conflict between Israelis and Palestinians is often seen as a cultural and religious battle between Judaism and Islam.*

An American Sikh family in New York. People need to feel that they can dress according to their culture, without fear of being attacked for looking different.

Fear of Islam exists in many countries with a Muslim minority, such as the United States, Britain, France, and Spain. Stereotypes about Islam are common—for example, that it is a cruel religion. Other myths are that all Muslims are terrorists, or that they take their religion to extremes.

Some people do not say that they hate other ethnic groups because it is not acceptable to admit that you are prejudiced. Instead, they talk about "cultural differences." For example, in the 1990s, Jean-Marie Le Pen, leader of the extreme right-wing National Front in France, argued that it is impossible for people from Western and non-Western cultures to live happily together because they are so different.

"At school they would say, 'Are you a terrorist?' And I would say, 'No, I am from Libya' and they would say, 'Yes, from Colonel Gaddafi' and I would say, 'No, from Libya. He is just the president there.'"
Sarina, 18, whose parents moved to Great Britain from Libya

We Don't Trust You

Today, Roma, or Gypsies, remain one of the largest ethnic minorities in Europe. The Roma have no national homeland; since migrating westward from India in the 10th century, they have spread from Asia Minor to virtually all the countries of Europe, including Ireland and Great Britain, and even to the Americas and Australia. Estimates of the current Roma population in Europe vary greatly, from 2 million to 5 million.

Gypsies have traditionally resisted complete participation in the societies of the countries where they settled.

FACT:
The six largest Roma populations in Europe
Romania   2,100,000
Bulgaria   750,000
Spain   725,000
Hungary   575,000
Slovakia   500,000
Turkey   400,000
Donal Kenrick, An Historical Dictionary of the Gypsy People, quoted by the Refugee Council, 1998

▼ *An elderly Roma couple in Granada, Spain.*

And both in the past and in the present, these societies have rarely welcomed Gypsies. Some 400,000 Roma were murdered by the Nazis during World War II. In the last decade, again there has been an increase in violence against Roma in Eastern Europe.

▶ *Czech Roma protesting against a wall built to separate them from other people, October 1999.*

case study · case study · case study · case study · case study

Josef is a Roma refugee from Slovakia. His family had homes, cars, and money there, but they were forced to flee. In Slovakia, the Roma are blamed for crimes they did not commit. They are attacked by gangs of skinheads, helped by the police. The skinheads wear boots with black laces. If they have beaten up lots of Roma, they wear white laces instead, like a medal.

Josef was attacked one afternoon by a group of skinheads. A week later he saw the leader of the group in police uniform. He went to the police station and told the officers about this, but they did not investigate. Then the police called him in and questioned him about various crimes. They beat him up, too.

Josef fled with his family to Great Britain in 1997. He now lives in Dover. Life is not easy for them because many people in Dover are prejudiced against Roma.

4. Scapegoating as a Form of Prejudice

What Is Scapegoating?

Sometimes a group of people is wrongly blamed for causing problems. This is called scapegoating. For instance, immigrants who do not have much money may move into an area where housing is run-down and there are not enough jobs. Some locals think that their situation will get worse because the newcomers will compete with them for housing and jobs. The lack of houses and work are not the immigrants' fault. Usually problems like those exist long before the arrival of the immigrants. Yet people may develop racist attitudes toward them, and some might even attack them.

When Idi Amin came to power in Uganda in 1971, he scapegoated the Ugandan Asians, an ethnic minority group, for all the country's problems. He said the Asians controlled too much of the economy. Many Africans were willing to believe that the Asians were taking the country's wealth, and they were pleased when Amin forced them out in 1972.

There are about 25 million ethnic Chinese people living in Southeast Asian countries. In some places they have been scapegoated because governments fear they have too much economic power.

▼ *Rioters in Medan in northern Sumatra, Indonesia, burning motorcycles stolen from a shop owned by ethnic Chinese people, May 1998.*

At times of economic and political crisis, racist policies have been directed against them. In the worst cases they have been forced out of the country. In May 1998, the Chinese community was scapegoated for the problems in Indonesia and suffered vicious attacks. At least 2,000 people were killed in Jakarta, the capital, alone.

In the United States, for example, Hispanic immigrants are often accused of taking jobs away from African Americans and other minority groups. Another example is Louis Farrakhan, leader of the African-American organization the Nation of Islam, which teaches that all Jews are evil and are primarily responsible for the problems of African Americans.

"Maybe the separation [of the races] might be the best answer."
Louis Farrakhan, March 1997

▼ *Louis Farrakhan speaking to hundreds of thousands of marchers who participated in the Million Man March to Washington, DC, in 1995.*

"Keep Them Out!"

What do you do if you cannot live in your country anymore, when you are being attacked because of your skin color, culture, religion, or political views? You will probably seek refuge in a nearby country. But being a refugee in a country in the European Union, for example, may be difficult as well. Many refugees in the European Union (EU) are victims of the wars in the former USSR and Yugoslavia who have lost their homes and jobs.

Refugees in the European Union are often:
• Separated from the rest of the population
• Placed in hostels
• Not allowed to work
• Given coupons instead of money to buy food (this happens in Switzerland, Germany, and Great Britain)

◀ *A man being arrested after a neo-Nazi attack on a hostel for refugees in Rostock, Germany, in 1993. The number of racist attacks in Germany is increasing today.*

These policies can lead to scapegoating. The new arrivals are seen as "scroungers" who are getting something for nothing. Throughout the 1990s there were racist attacks on hostels in countries such as Germany, Holland, Sweden, and Austria. Often, the racists try to burn down the buildings—sometimes with the people still inside.

▶ *A Vietnamese woman and child fleeing Communist Vietnam on a fishing boat. Immigrants also fled Vietnam by boat to escape racism.*

case study · case study · case study · case study · case study

In 1978, Chinese immigrants began to leave Vietnam after anti-Chinese prejudice increased. Most fled to other Southeast Asian countries. From 1979 to 1992, small numbers of Vietnamese refugees were allowed to enter Australia, Canada, the United States, and Europe.

Quang Bui's brother escaped from Vietnam by boat. It was a dangerous voyage, and many died of thirst or drowned in the rough seas. After a long and difficult journey, Quang Bui's brother reached Sweden and was allowed to settle there as a refugee. Quang Bui and his parents were later able to join him.

When he first arrived, Quang Bui was called "yellow neck" and other racist names by older Swedish boys. Vietnamese kids stood up to them and helped Quang Bui, but he still felt threatened and afraid a lot of the time. Today, Quang Bui teaches workshops to children and adults. He uses his own life history to illustrate how painful racism can be to those who experience it.

Prejudice and the Media

The pictures we see in the newspapers and on TV can influence the way we view people from other countries and cultures. For example, if you only see Africans starving in village shacks or fighting wars, you may not know about the millions who live in apartments or houses like you and go to work or school each day. This lack of information can lead to stereotyping of other peoples.

For many years, films in the United States presented a stereotyped view of African Americans, Chinese people, and Native Americans. Black people were never shown as important, powerful, or clever. The Chinese were portrayed as cruel and not to be trusted, and Native Americans as savages who killed white people.

Spike Lee (left) has made many movies showing the lives of African Americans. His work has helped to create a new respect for African-American cinema and has encouraged black actors and directors to discuss racial issues.

Things are getting better, but there still is a long way to go. There are now more black and Hispanic actors in the United States making programs showing non-white people in a wide range of roles. Publishers have begun to focus on producing multicultural books to avoid stereotyping. Many of the larger publishers in the United States are even publishing books in languages other than English to avoid an "English-only" point of view.

Yet prejudice can sometimes be aggravated by the media. In many European countries, newspapers brand asylum seekers as people making "bogus" asylum claims and "flooding" the country. A writer for the *Irish Times* found that in 2000 nearly all the local newspapers in Ireland wrote bad things about the asylum seekers moving into their area. The newcomers are often scapegoated for society's problems, such as unemployment. Words written in the papers can encourage attacks on the streets.

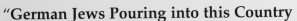

"**German Jews Pouring into this Country**
The way stateless Jews from Germany are pouring into this country is becoming an outrage."
The Daily Mail, *newspaper, London, August 20, 1938*

"**Why Do We Let in This Army of Spongers?**
So many asylum seekers are pouring into this country...that the authorities here are finding that they simply can't cope."
The Daily Mail, *newspaper, London, September 26, 1998*

▲ *Workers from the Refugee Arrivals Project help asylum seekers at Heathrow Airport in England. Many asylum seekers arrive alone after a long and difficult journey and do not speak English.*

5. Institutional Racism

What Is Institutional Racism?

Institutional racism occurs when the way a society is organized results in the members of a group receiving unequal treatment rather than being judged fairly as individuals. Institutional racism is often the result of longstanding behavior and beliefs that lead to racist results, even when such prejudice and discrimination may be expressly forbidden by law.

An example of institutional racism in the United States is the public school system in many places. Until the middle of the 20th century, segregation—the separation of the races in public places—was the law in the United States. In 1954, the Supreme Court ruled that segregation in public education was illegal. Over time, the result was an end of the *legal* system of segregated education. However,

FACT:
41.9 percent of African-American children live below the poverty line.
Institute for Jewish Policy Research and American Jewish Committee, 1998

◀ *Hispanic farm workers come to the United States to work, but have few rights. In the 1960s, a man named Cesar Chavez gave hope to workers by organizing them and creating the National Farm Workers Association (NFWA).*

case study · case study · case study · case study · case study

One consequence of institutional racism in public education in the United States is that members of some minorities are less likely to graduate from high school or be admitted to college and graduate school. To combat this likelihood, some colleges and graduate schools give special consderation to minority applicants. Opponents of such programs, which are often referred to as "affirmative action," argue that they are a form of reverse discrimination. Supporters argue that such programs are necessary to undo the effects of institutional racism.

recent studies have shown that in most places in the United States, public education is effectively as segregated as ever. How can this be?

Public school districts are drawn by neighborhood. For many reasons, blacks tend to live in predominantly black neighborhoods, and whites in mostly white neighborhoods. The result is public schools that are either mostly white or mostly black—still segregated, in effect, although deliberate segregation is illegal.

▶ *In 2001, Colin Powell gained the important job of U.S. Secretary of State.*

"We Were Here First"

Australia's Cathy Freeman carrying both the Aboriginal and Australian flags after winning the women's 400-meter final at the Sydney Olympic Games in 2000.

Native peoples in some countries face problems because their lands are run by other people who see them as inferior. It is hard for them to find a good home and make a living in their own land. How did this system of prejudice come about?

It has historical roots. For example, in the 19th century, European settlers went to Australia and took land from the Aborigines. At the same time, the Native Americans of North America were removed from their land and forced to live on reservations. In the 20th century, European settlers in South Africa brought in a system of laws called apartheid (an Afrikaans word meaning "separation") to discriminate against the native Africans.

The settlers thought this behavior was acceptable because they viewed the native peoples as primitive savages and unable to rule themselves. In many countries, this attitude can still be found.

◀ *A Maya teacher with students in Guatemala. Since the 1980s many schools have been set up to teach the Maya in their own language.*

The native Maya of Central America were almost wiped out by Spanish invaders in the 16th century. They have remained at the bottom of society ever since. The Maya own little land in countries that were once theirs, and most live in poverty. In the 1980s at least 20,000 of them were killed by the Guatemalan army during a civil war fought over land and human rights. The Maya still suffer institutional racism because of their low position in society. They are often ignored when they go to government hospitals for treatment. People overcharge them in shops and on buses. Non-native people from their own countries tell them that they are lazy and dirty, and need "civilizing."

"You can't teach the Indians anything. How many times have we tried to improve their way of life? They just won't change."
Typical comment about the Maya quoted by the Minority Rights Group, Great Britain, 1994

Effects of Institutional Racism

What are the consequences of the kind of institutional racism in public education discussed on pages 28–29? This is a very complex issue, with few simple answers, that is the subject of much political debate in the United States and elsewhere.

Perhaps the only point on which a consensus, or general agreement, can be said to have been reached is that unequal educational opportunity in early life results in unequal quality of life later on. Whether it be in the United States or anywhere else, poverty and lack of education go together. The poorest members of society are almost always the least educated. Linked to poverty and lack of education are a number of other serious problems. These include a higher occurrence of drug and alcohol abuse; greater frequency of domestic abuse; greater likelihood of being the victim of a violent crime; higher rates of divorce, separation, or other forms of family breakup; greater likelihood of involvement in criminal activity and of being imprisoned; less access

▼ *Muslim schoolgirls at Al-Ghazaly school in Jersey City, New Jersey. In some places, Muslims have set up their own schools so that their children do not suffer from racism at school.*

to medical care; higher death rate at all ages and a shorter life span.

In the United States, the minority groups that are most likely to be affected by the consequences of institutional racism in public education are African Americans and Hispanics. For a number of reasons, both groups are among the poorest in American society, and unequal educational opportunity makes it more likely that such poverty will endure.

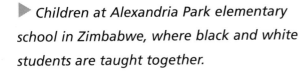 *Children at Alexandria Park elementary school in Zimbabwe, where black and white students are taught together.*

FACT:
In the United States, about two-thirds of the money given to students for a college education is in the form of loans. According to sociologist Derek Price, white students are more willing to take out such loans, believing that they are likely to get a good job eventually that will allow them to repay the money. Fewer black students apply for such loans, in part because they are aware that they are less likely than white students to get a high-paying job in the future—a subtle example of institutional racism.

6. Feeling Superior

How Can Nationalism Lead to Prejudice?

Are you proud of your country? Many people feel attached to the land where they were born, and are proud of its culture and history—they are nationalists. But nationalism can lead some people to believe they have more of a right to live in their country than other people who were not born there. They feel superior to the newcomers.

This feeling is more common if the new arrivals come from a different ethnic group or culture. It can lead to prejudice toward them. White immigrants from Europe, Canada, and Australia have rarely had problems settling in the United States. Yet Indian, African, Asian, and Hispanic immigrants have suffered from racism.

▶ *Citizens wave the American flag at a parade in New York City. Nationalism can bring people together, but it can also turn them against outsiders.*

Even minority groups who have lived in another country for generations may experience racism. The Koreans are the largest ethnic minority in Japan. They suffer discrimination in housing and jobs, even if they have lived there all their lives. Many Japanese feel superior to the Koreans and also to black immigrants, believing that they simply do not fit into their society.

> "Many sangokujin [third-world people] and other foreigners who have entered Japan illegally have repeatedly committed atrocious crimes. In the event of a major earthquake, even riots may break out."
>
> *Tokyo governor Shintaro Ishihara, April 9, 2000*

In fact, most countries are made up of a mixture of different cultures, ethnic groups, and religions. But racists tend to believe that their country has only one true culture. For example, the idea of the United States as a land made up only by the sons and daughters of pilgrims is a false one. One of the principal traits of the United States has always been that it is made up of many different cultures. But it is always easier to blame others for all of society's problems.

▼ *Workers from the Philippines in Kuwait City, Kuwait. Many Filipinos work as servants in the Gulf States to make money to send home to their families.*

"We're Better than You"

If a person can't make a good living in his or her own country, he or she may decide to move abroad. Since World War II, there has been mass migration from the poorer to the richer regions of the world.

Immigrants are needed to fill jobs—often the badly paid jobs that no one else wants to do. Some people, when they see the newcomers sweeping the streets or cleaning the toilets, may feel they are superior to them. In this way racist views can start to spread.

FACT:
The number of whites in the United States dropped from approximately 83.7 percent in 1991 to 71.3 percent in 2000. The population in 2000 was: whites, 196.9 million; African Americans, 33.6 million; Hispanics, 32.8 million; Asians, 10.6 million; Native Americans, 2 million.
U.S. Government Report, 2000

◀ *Mexican food stalls with signs in Spanish and English in San Antonio, Texas. Many people whose families come from Mexico live in San Antonio, so several of the stores there sell Mexican food.*

Out of 100 million Mexicans, around 40 million live in poverty. About 7 million of them live in the United States, mostly doing low-paying jobs. Some white Americans may feel that Mexican customs, food, and the Spanish language—which they believe are inferior to their own—are "swamping" their country. They find it hard to accept that they live in a nation made up of many cultures. This results in anti-Mexican racism.

The U.S. and European economies need well-qualified immigrants, such as computer programmers from India. Yet some people, who believe that immigrants from poor countries are inferior, find it hard to accept the newcomers even though they are highly skilled and valuable to society.

▼ *These computer users in Bangalore, India, may one day use their skills working in the United States or Europe.*

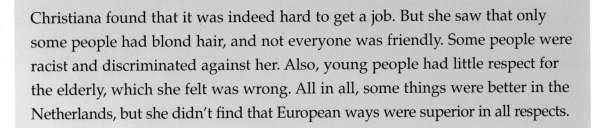

case study · case study · case study · case study · case study

Christiana Kwarteng and her family moved to the Netherlands from Ghana. Before she arrived, she thought that all Dutch people were blond and friendly. She believed that they spoke German, lived freely, and were rich. She thought it would be hard to find work there.

Christiana found that it was indeed hard to get a job. But she saw that only some people had blond hair, and not everyone was friendly. Some people were racist and discriminated against her. Also, young people had little respect for the elderly, which she felt was wrong. All in all, some things were better in the Netherlands, but she didn't find that European ways were superior in all respects.

Fascism Rears Its Ugly Head

After the horrors of World War II, why are there still fascists today? It seems there will always be some people who feel that their ethnic group is superior to all others. There are fascist organizations around the world, notably in Europe, the United States, South Africa, and India.

In some European countries, including Austria, Germany, France, Denmark, and Belgium, fascist parties have gained some political power. Their members do not openly say they are racist. Instead they talk about protecting their national culture. They refer to the problem of poverty and argue that money should be spent on local people whose families have always lived there—usually meaning white people. This argument appeals to some voters; it is easy to blame immigrants for problems in society that are actually quite complicated.

> "As more immigrants bring their children into western Europe, the indigenous population is slowly being substituted by aliens."
>
> *Jörg Haider, Governor of Carinthia, Austria, 1995*

► *Jörg Haider, leader of the extreme-right Freedom Party in Austria.*

In the United States there are small fascist groups. They do not have political power, but they are active in other ways. They attack African Americans, Asian Americans, Jews, Koreans, and homosexuals. They set fire to their homes or vandalize their property. Between 1988 and 1999 at least 49 murders were committed by U.S. fascists.

In India, the Bharatiya Janata Party (BJP) believes Hinduism is the true religion of India. It aims to force the country to accept Hindu laws, although 100 million Indians, 11 percent of the population, are Muslim. In states where the party has been elected, the BJP has scapegoated Muslims. In Bombay, Bangladeshi Muslims who have lived in India for years have been accused of taking jobs from Indians. The government has deported them back to Bangladesh. To try to "persuade" them not to return, police officers have often beaten the men and raped the women.

Muslims who have tied a Hindu man to a handcart pulling him through the streets of Bombay, India, during the 1992 riots. The riots started after extremist Hindus destroyed the Ayodhya mosque.

7. What Can We Do?

How Can People End Prejudice?

Throughout history, wherever there has been racism, there have always been people who have fought against it. These people have sometimes been able to bring about social change.

African Americans did not get treated equally in the United States even after slavery ended in 1865. They were paid lower wages and had poorer homes and schools. They were also segregated, which meant that they could not live in the same places or use the same facilities as whites. In the 1960s many black and white people joined the civil rights movement. This massive campaign of meetings, marches, and demonstrations forced the government to change the laws to make them fairer to black people. It did not solve all of the

▼ *The Reverend Martin Luther King, Jr., one of the main leaders of the civil rights movement, is shown with leaders of the 1965 march from Selma to Montgomery, Alabama.*

FACT:
Montgomery, Alabama, 1955: Rosa Parks, an African-American woman tired after her day's work, sat down in the only remaining seat— in the whites-only part of the bus. A white man demanded to sit down but she refused to get up. This began the Montgomery bus boycott, and the start of the civil rights movement.

problems, but it was a big step in the right direction.

One of the greatest recent struggles was the fight against apartheid in South Africa. In 1948, the South African government brought in the apartheid system. This meant it divided its people into separate "races," giving whites the most rights and black Africans the fewest. Black people could not mix with white people; they had separate schools, towns, buses—and even park benches. Most lived in poverty. The struggle against this unfair system included demonstrations, strikes, and guerrilla war. Many ordinary people from all around the world supported the struggle against apartheid. Apartheid was overthrown in the early 1990s when South Africa elected its first black president, Nelson Mandela.

▲ In 1994, South African President Nelson Mandela addressed a crowd at a meeting in memory of the student protests against apartheid in 1976. The banner shows Hector Peterson, a student who died in the protests.

In Australia, Aborigines have battled to win equal rights with the white population. In the 1960s, young Aborigines started their own civil rights movement. They took a new pride in their Aborigine lifestyle and culture. Their main campaign was to win back the land that was taken from them during European settlement. Finally, in 1993, Prime Minister Paul Keating agreed with their claim and Aborigines began to recover land.

Organizing and Protesting

If racists started to harass a family living in your neighborhood, would you help to support that family? Stopping racism is not always a huge struggle against a political power like the apartheid government in South Africa. The first step can be to simply speak out against racism.

Many people, both black and white, are horrified by racism and will take to the streets to protest against it. In Austria, large numbers of people were shocked when Jörg Haider, leader of the far-right Freedom Party, came in second in the national elections of October 1999. The Freedom Party has its roots in the Austrian Nazi Party, which ruled the country during World War II. Thousands of Austrians protested against Haider's party. They feared that the success of this fascist organization would lead to growing racism in their country.

◀ A demonstration in Belgium following the electoral success of Jörg Haider's Freedom Party in Austria. The middle poster says "Fascism never again" and calls for the stopping of Vlaams Blok, a Belgian far-right political party.

In 1992, Rodney King was brutally beaten by policemen in Los Angeles, California. When the police were acquitted of criminal charges in the incident, days of rioting followed.

> "[I came] to make a symbolic gesture and try to give another picture of Germany."
>
> *Flavia-Victoria Mai, a supporter of an anti-Nazi demonstration of about 200,000 people in Berlin, Germany, November 2000*

An event that shocked many people in the United States was the 1999 murder of Amadou Diallo, an African immigrant in New York City. Diallo was shot 41 times in the lobby of his apartment building by undercover New York City police officers, who regarded his presence and behavior as "suspicious."

The incident was one of several in New York City that made some people wonder whether the police were too quick to resort to deadly force, especially in interaction with members of minority groups. Many people also asked whether Diallo's death was the result of what is known as "racial profiling"—the targeting by the police of certain minority groups, especially African Americans, as more likely to be guilty of criminal behavior.

How Can We Help?

▼ *Ian Wright, soccer player for England.*

If you hear prejudiced remarks or jokes, or there is racist bullying at your school, you can try doing some or all of these things:

• Speak out. If you say nothing, others may think you agree
• Invite speakers from different communities to help to break down prejudice
• Organize discussions about human rights and racism
• Form a school policy against racism
• Join an anti-racist or human rights organization

Athletics can be a great way of breaking down racism. In the United States, the most famous athlete in this regard is Jackie Robinson. In 1947, as a second baseman for the Brooklyn Dodgers, Robinson became the first African American in baseball's Major Leagues. Prior to Robinson's debut, all

"
"A life is not important except in the impact it has on other lives."
—*Epitaph on Jackie Robinson's gravestone, written by himself*
"

professional sports in the United States had been segregated. Robinson went on to win election to the Baseball Hall of Fame; since that time, black athletes have dominated the major professional sports—baseball, football, and basketball—in the United States.

It's up to all of us to do what we can. We would all be happier in a society free from the fear, distrust, ignorance, and prejudice that cause racism.

▶ *Having friends from different cultures makes life richer and more interesting.*

case study · case study · case study · case study · case study

Mary Seacole Comprehensive Girls' School in the Midlands, England, has students from many backgrounds. Just under half are from south Asian families, a third are white, and about 18 percent are Afro-Caribbean. To tackle the problem of racism, the students were involved in making an anti-racist policy. Some of the teachers weren't agreeable at first, but the girls' enthusiasm persuaded them that change was needed.

Now, the students often deal with racist incidents themselves. As Robina says, "We find if people are racist…that the person [making the comments] is isolated. You know, even their own friends will isolate that person." Most of the white girls take the issue just as seriously. All of the girls talk about the benefits of knowing people from different cultures and religions. They are more confident about questioning other things that go on in school, too.

GLOSSARY

Abused
Insulted or attacked.

Anti-Semitism
Hatred of Jewish people, which by the late 19th century had become a new kind of hatred based on ideas about "race."

Apartheid
"Apartness." The apartheid system was brought in by the white South African government in 1948. It kept white, black, and mixed-race peoples separate and unequal.

Asylum
The right to live in another country if you are under attack in your own. People who suffer because of their skin color, culture, religion, or political beliefs often flee to other countries to try to claim this right. They are called asylum seekers.

Boycott
To get together with other people and refuse to have anything to do with a company, group of people, or foreign country.

British National Party (BNP)
A far-right political party in Great Britain, formed in the 1980s, which supports racial discrimination and is against immigration.

Civil rights
The rights of people in a country to live freely and equally, whatever their ethnic group or personal views.

Civil war
War between two or more groups of people within a country.

Coalition government
A government formed from more than one political party.

Colonialism
When one country rules another land as if it owned it.

Deport
To send a person back to the country from which he or she came.

Discrimination
Treating a group of people worse than other groups.

Ethnic group
A group of people who share a common culture, tradition, and perhaps language.

Ethnic minority
A group of people who have a different culture, religion, language, or skin color from most other people in their society.

European Union (EU)
An organization of western European countries that trade together and try to agree on certain common policies, for example, how they deal with asylum seekers.

Fascism
An extreme right-wing system of government based on the belief that one country or ethnic group is better than all others, and the need to obey one powerful leader.

Fascist
A person who believes that his or her country or ethnic group is better than all others, and obeys a powerful leader.

Genetics
The study of how physical features are passed on from parents to their offspring.

Ghettos
Parts of a city, especially very poor areas, where minority groups tend to live.

Guerrilla war
War fought by bands of fighters against a regular army.

Harass
To keep troubling and annoying someone.

Hispanics
Spanish-speaking people living in the United States, whose families come from Latin America.

Ignorant
Not knowing about a subject.

Immigrants
People who enter another country to live there.

Ku Klux Klan
An extreme right-wing secret society, founded in the southern states of the United States in the 1860s to oppose giving rights to black people. It still exists today. The KKK attacks Jews and non-whites.

Migration
The movement of people from one country to another.

Nazis
Supporters of Adolf Hitler's Nazi Party in Germany in the 1930s and 1940s.

Pensioners
People who no longer work and who receive money to live on, called a pension, usually from the government.

Primitive
Simple, undeveloped.

Raped
Forced to have sex.

Reservations
Areas, usually of poor land, where Native Americans were forced to live after they were forced off their territories in the 19th century.

Stereotype
Something that is said about a whole group of people, such as "All Jews are rich." A stereotype is not based on fact and is insulting. It means people from that group are seen as all the same and not as individuals.

Vandalize
To damage or destroy buildings deliberately.

Xenophobia
Hatred of people from other countries.

FURTHER INFORMATION

BOOKS TO READ

Beals, Melba Patillo. *Warriors Don't Cry: A Searing Memoir of the Battle to Integrate Little Rock's Central High* (Abridged Edition). New York: Archway, 1995.

Colbert, Jan (ed). *Dear Dr. King: Letters from Today's Children to Dr. Martin Luther King, Jr.* New York: Jump at the Sun, 2000.

Counts, Will. *A Life is More Than A Moment: The Desegregation of Little Rock's Central High.* Bloomington: Indiana University Press, 1999.

Haskins, James. *The Day Martin Luther King, Jr., Was Shot: A Photo History of the Civil Rights Movement.* Topeka: Econo-Clad Books, 1999.

Levine, Ellen. *Freedom's Children: Young Civil Rights Activists Tell Their Own Stories.* New York: Puffin, 2000.

Medearis, Angela Shelf. *Dare To Dream: Coretta Scott King and the Civil Rights Movement.* New York: Puffin, 1998.

Naylor, Phyliis Reynolds. *Walker's Crossing.* New York: Aladdin Paperbacks, 2001.

Reed, Gregory J. and Rosa Parks. *Dear Mrs. Parks: A Dialogue With Today's Youth.* New York: Lee & Low Books, 1997.

Taylor, Mildred D. and Jerry Pinkney. *Roll of Thunder, Hear My Cry.* New York: Phyllis Fogelman Books, 2001.

Turck, Mary. *The Civil Rights Movement for Kids: A History with 21 Activities.* Chicago: Chicago Review Press, 2000.

WEBSITES

http://www.familywonder.com/13up/a/
20000117MalcolmX.html
This website is designed for teachers, parents, and kids. Answer questions about racism, prejudices, and more in order to prompt discussions and debates.

www.dosomething.org
This website encourages kids to speak up, participate, and take action on issues that are important to them.

ORGANIZATIONS

International Organization for the Study of Human Rights in the United States
(EAFORD)
2025 Eye Street NW, Suite 1120
Washington, DC 20006

INDEX